COOKING IN BURGUNDY AND CHAMPAGNE

Many people consider these two territories as being blessed by God. Those who appreciate good wine and good food – and everything that has to do with them – know that there are few other places anywhere in the world where Mother Nature has so generously bestowed so many of her gifts. These marvels are found in Burgundy in particular, but also Champagne, the home of the vineyards that produce that nectar that has always made the dreams of men, connoisseurs and non, Frenchmen and citizens of the world – and fortunately continues to do so. These two regions of France, while geographically contiguous, have quite dissimilar points of view in many respects – actually, in just about all respects. It is enough to think of how wine – and what wine! – is produced in Burgundy and in Champagne to explain many of the differences. There are those who disparagingly insist that the first, with no sparkle, is a laical creation exalted by the potentates of old, the Dukes of Burgundy, and that champagne was instead invented in the blessed cellars of the abbeys; and they go further yet, claiming as its greatest *défenseur* – or sponsor, in modern-day terms – no less than pope Urban II. It is not by chance that the windows of Notre-Dame d'Épernay narrate the life of Bacchus and not that of Jesus, who, they say, must not have been much of a connoisseur if he transformed water into wine and then served it immediately, without allowing it to stand for even an hour! But leaving aside all these more or less ideological disputes, Burgundy is also well-blessed – with its meats and vegetables, its snails and its extraordinary fowl, its *moutardes* and its sauces, certain excellent white wines (like Chablis and Mersault, Puligny-Montrachet and Corton-Charlemagne), and of course the whole family of red wines, from the Côtes de Nuits to the Côtes de Beaune, that merit one adjective only: unforgettable.

A WORD FROM THE NUTRITIONIST

The great culinary traditions of these regions may well be defined as typically northern European. The fats used in this type of cooking are mainly lard, bacon fat, fresh cream, and butter – in short, fats of animal origin and therefore abounding in saturated fatty acids. The meats are also often anything but lean, and are just as often cooked in what might appear to be enormous quantities of wine or other alcoholic liquids – perhaps only naturally, given the excellent wine-making traditions of these regions. All this makes for delicious but extremely rich fare.
So "Bon appetit!" – but watch your calories and your cholesterol count!

Eggs in Wine ▶

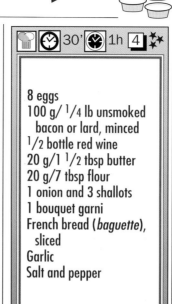

While stirring constantly, brown the flour lightly in the melted butter. Add the bacon, the bouquet garni, the wine, 1/3 cup water, the minced onion and shallots, and salt and pepper to taste. Cook for 30–40 minutes. Remove the bouquet garni and strain the sauce. Fill 4 individual ovenproof dishes to 2/3 full. Break 2 eggs into each and bake at 200°C/375°F until the whites are cooked but the yolks are still liquid.

Sprinkle with pepper and serve with slices of French bread rubbed with garlic.

🍳 ⏱ 30' ⏰ 1h 4 ✴✴

8 eggs
100 g/ 1/4 lb unsmoked
    bacon or lard, minced
1/2 bottle red wine
20 g/1 1/2 tbsp butter
20 g/7 tbsp flour
1 onion and 3 shallots
1 bouquet garni
French bread (*baguette*),
    sliced
Garlic
Salt and pepper

Kcal 490 P 26 G 24 ⚖

Snails in Wine Sauce

Pour the red wine into a capacious pan and add the chopped shallots. Boil over high heat until reduced by three-quarters.

Add the beef stock, bring to a boil, and reduce again by three-quarters. Strain the sauce and replace the pan on the stove over low heat.

Add the butter a little at a time while beating with a whisk. Season to taste with salt and pepper. "Drown" the snails in the sauce and reheat to just below boiling.

To serve, arrange the snails on individual serving plates, accompanied by the sauce.

🍳 ⏱ 6' ⏰ 20' 4 ✴

4 dozen canned snails
2 liters/8 cups red wine
2 liters/8 cups beef stock
250 g/ 1/2 lb shallots
200 g/ 7/8 cup butter
Salt and pepper

Kcal 771 P 18 G 57 ⚖

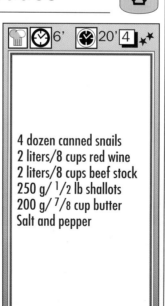

Potatoes and Mushrooms

M elt 1 tablespoon of the butter and add the diced bacon. Cook for 2 minutes, then add the thyme leaves, the bay leaf, and the minced shallots. Dust with the flour, mix well, and cook for 3 minutes longer. Add the wine and bring to a boil; add the peeled and diced potatoes and continue cooking over low heat for 20 minutes. In the meantime, melt the rest of the butter and sauté the mushrooms until they release all the moisture they contain. Drain and add to the potatoes. Cook for 10 minutes longer and adjust salt and pepper.

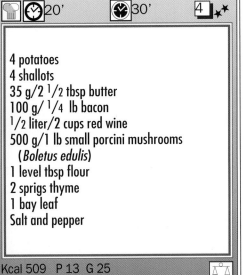

🍲 🕐 20' ⊛ 30' 4 ★★

4 potatoes
4 shallots
35 g/2 1/2 tbsp butter
100 g/ 1/4 lb bacon
1/2 liter/2 cups red wine
500 g/1 lb small porcini mushrooms
    (*Boletus edulis*)
1 level tbsp flour
2 sprigs thyme
1 bay leaf
Salt and pepper

Kcal 509 P 13 G 25

Chicken Liver Terrine

O n the evening of the day before, place the cut-up chicken livers, the chopped onion and shallot, the crushed garlic, the parsley, and the *marc* in a lidded earthenware terrine. Cover and allow to stand in a cool place overnight. The next day, soak the bread for a few minutes in the milk; squeeze out the excess liquid and place on a cutting board together with all the ingredients in the terrine and the cut-up pork jowl. Chop until very fine. Add the eggs and salt and pepper to taste; mix well. Pack into the terrine and arrange the 10 bay leaves on the surface. Cover. Set in a larger pan of water. Bake in a preheated 280°C/525°F oven for 15–20 minutes; reduce the heat to 200°C/375°F and continue baking for 1 1/4 hours. Remove the terrine from the oven and pour the boiling aspic over it. Allow the aspic to set before serving.

🍲 🕐 40'+12h ⊛ 1h 6 ★★

500 g/1 lb chicken livers
700 g/1 1/2 lbs pork jowl
1/2 liter/2 cups hot aspic
2 eggs
1 thick slice day-old bread
10 tbsp milk
1 onion and 1 shallot
1 clove garlic
1 tbsp minced parsley
10 bay leaves
1 shot glass *marc de Bourgogne* (brandy)
Salt and pepper

Kcal 1158 P 173 G 23

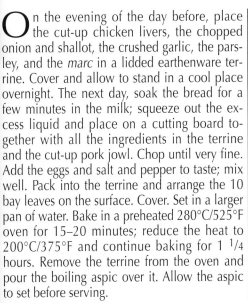

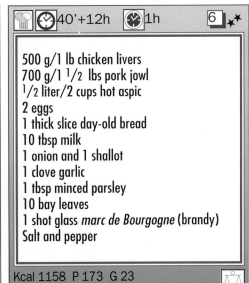

Green Onion Pie

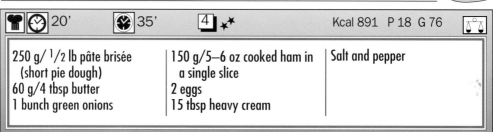

🍳🕐 20'	⏲ 35'	4 ⋆⋆		Kcal 891 P 18 G 76	⚖

250 g/ ¹/₂ lb pâte brisée (short pie dough) 60 g/4 tbsp butter 1 bunch green onions	150 g/5–6 oz cooked ham in a single slice 2 eggs 15 tbsp heavy cream	Salt and pepper

1 Line a well-buttered ovenproof pan with the pâte brisée, rolled to 5 mm thickness (a little over ¹/₈ in). Prick the dough generously with a fork and allow to stand in a cool place.

2 Cut off the green leaves of the onions, rinse thoroughly, cut into thin slices, and chop. Skin and slice the bulbs. Melt the rest of the butter and sauté the sliced onion until soft.

3 Add the chopped leaves, season with salt and pepper to taste, and cook for 3 minutes longer.

4 Remove the pan from the heat and allow to cool somewhat. Add the beaten eggs and the cream, and blend thoroughly. Pour the mixture into the pie shell, top with the diced cooked ham, and bake at 180°C/350°F for 30 minutes.

Fried Ham with Tarragon Sauce

Melt the lard slowly over low heat in frying pan. Trim the fat from the ham slices and reserve. Sauté the ham slices, turning once, and remove from the heat. In a saucepan, melt the butter and blend in the flour; cook for 3 minutes, stirring constantly. Add the wine a little at a time, while continuing to stir so that a uniform consistency is obtained. Blend in the chicken stock and continue to cook over low heat. In the meantime, make a fine mince of the ham fat and add to the mixture in the saucepan, together with the crushed juniper berries and the tarragon. Allow to cook and thicken for 15 minutes.
In another saucepan, boil the vinegar with the crushed peppercorns, uncovered, for 10 minutes. Pour the contents of the first saucepan into the second and cook over low heat for 15 minutes.
Add the cream, adjust the salt, and keep warm. Return the ham slices to the frying pan and heat through. Serve hot on individual plates with the strained sauce.

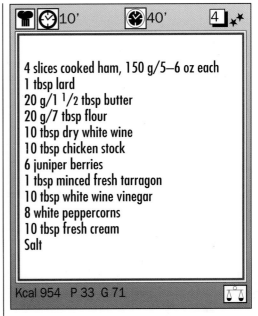

🍴🕐 10' ⏱ 40' 4 ★★

4 slices cooked ham, 150 g/5–6 oz each
1 tbsp lard
20 g/1 1/2 tbsp butter
20 g/7 tbsp flour
10 tbsp dry white wine
10 tbsp chicken stock
6 juniper berries
1 tbsp minced fresh tarragon
10 tbsp white wine vinegar
8 white peppercorns
10 tbsp fresh cream
Salt

Kcal 954 P 33 G 71

Ham with Parsley

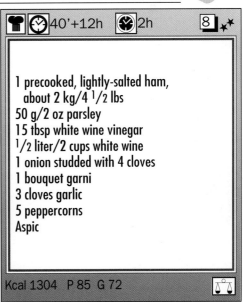

Prepare a court bouillon with the white wine, 3 liters/3 quarts water, the clove-studded onion, the bouquet garni, the garlic, and the peppercorns.
Simmer the ham in the liquid, covered, for a generous two hours. Soak the minced parsley in the vinegar for at least 15 minutes.
Remove the ham from the court-bouillon, and when cool enough to handle, cut the meat into small, uniform pieces.
Cover the bottom of a terrine with little of the aspic. Alternate layers of ham and parsley until the ingredients are used up. Press well and cover with aspic (the quantity will depend on personal taste).
Weight the top of the terrine and refrigerate for at least 12 hours before serving.

🍴🕐 40'+12h ⏱ 2h 8 ★★

1 precooked, lightly-salted ham,
   about 2 kg/4 1/2 lbs
50 g/2 oz parsley
15 tbsp white wine vinegar
1/2 liter/2 cups white wine
1 onion studded with 4 cloves
1 bouquet garni
3 cloves garlic
5 peppercorns
Aspic

Kcal 1304 P 85 G 72

Potatoes Bresse Style ▶

Peel and finely slice the potatoes. In an ovenproof dish, melt 20 g/1 $^1/_2$ tablespoons of the butter. Make a layer of potatoes, cover with a layer of thinly sliced cheese, and continue in this manner until all the ingredients are used up. Pour in the hot stock and dot with the rest of the butter. Bake in a preheated 170°C/325°F oven per 1 $^1/_2$ hours. Should the surface risk browning too much, cover with a sheet of aluminum foil. Serve sprinkled with minced parsley.

🍳 ⏰ 15' ⏱ 1h+30' 6 ✶✶

1 kg/2 $^1/_4$ lbs potatoes
250 g/ $^1/_2$ lb Comté
   or Gruyère cheese
10 tbsp chicken stock
50 g/3 $^1/_2$ tbsp butter
1 tbsp minced parsley

Kcal 1523 P 28 G 132 ⚖

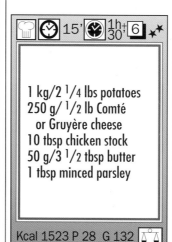

Snail Lasagna

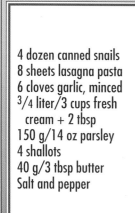

Heat $^3/_4$ liter/3 cups cream in a saucepan. Add the garlic and barely simmer for 10 minutes. Remove the garlic, mash with a fork, and replace in the hot cream. Press through a sieve.

Cook the shallots in the melted butter until softened. Blanch the parsley for 2 minutes, chop finely, and add to the pan together with the 2 tablespoons of cream; mix well and season very lightly with salt and pepper.

Cook the lasagne for 8 minutes in boiling salted water; drain and lay out on a cloth. Spread the parsley mixture on 4 of the lasagne arranged on a heated serving platter. Top with the snails. Lay the remaining 4 lasagne on top and cover with the garlic cream, reheated almost to boiling.

🍳 ⏰ 20' ⏱ 30' 4 ✶✶

4 dozen canned snails
8 sheets lasagna pasta
6 cloves garlic, minced
$^3/_4$ liter/3 cups fresh
   cream + 2 tbsp
150 g/14 oz parsley
4 shallots
40 g/3 tbsp butter
Salt and pepper

Kcal 864   P 24 G 70 ⚖

Snail Rolls

🍳⏰ 20'   ⚙ 30'   4 ✶✶   Kcal 303 P 24 G 15 ⚖

28 canned snails	¹/4 liter/1 cup chicken stock	and parsley)
1 Savoy cabbage	2 tbsp butter	Salt and pepper
2 cloves garlic	2 tbsp chopped herbs	
4 shallots, minced	(chives, tarragon, chervil	

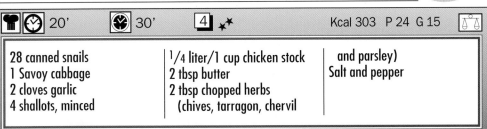

1 Remove the outer leaves of the cabbage. Blanch about 30 of the inner leaves in salted water, with the two unpeeled garlic cloves, for 3 minutes. Lift out the leaves and spread to drain.

3 Slide the snail rolls gently into the heated stock and simmer over very low heat until just warmed through. Arrange 7 rolls in each serving dish.

2 Cook the garlic for 2 minutes more, then remove and reserve. Cook the shallots in 1 tablespoon of the butter until soft. Place a spoonful of shallots and a snail in the center of each leaf and roll up.

4 Reduce the stock over high heat. Remove from the heat and add the mashed garlic, the chopped herbs, 1 tbsp butter, and salt and pepper to taste. Pour over the snail rolls and serve.

Baked Cheese ▶

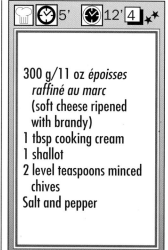

F ill four rather deep porcelain ovenproof molds two-thirds full with the cheese and bake for 12 minutes at 150°C/300°F.

Mix the cream with the finely-chopped shallot, the chives, and salt and pepper to taste. Top each cheese mold with a dab of the sauce and serve.

🍳⏱5' ⏰12'[4]✯✯

300 g/11 oz *époisses
raffiné au marc*
(soft cheese ripened
with brandy)
1 tbsp cooking cream
1 shallot
2 level teaspoons minced
chives
Salt and pepper

Kcal 321   P 23   G 24 ⚖

Chasource Cheese Pie

M ix the ingredients by hand or with an electric mixer; gather into a ball and allow to stand in a cool place for about one hour.

Heat the oven to 180°C/350°F. Roll out the dough and line a buttered and floured pie pan. Cover with a sheet of aluminum foil, fill with dried beans, and bake for 15 minutes. Beat the eggs; add the milk, the chives, and a dash of pepper. Slice the cheese and then cut each slice in two. Remove the beans and foil from the baked crust.

Lay the cheese slices, slightly overlapping, on the crust. Pour in the egg mixture, dust with paprika, and bake for 20 minutes. Serve this pie with a green salad.

🍳⏱30'+ ⏰35'[4]✯✯
     1h

For the crust:
250 g/2 ¹/₄ cups flour
+ 1 tbsp
125 g/9 tbsp butter
+ 1 tbsp
1 pinch salt
¹/₂ cup cold water

For the filling:
1 *chaource* cheese
(ca. 450 g/1 lb)
3 eggs
¹/₂ liter/2 cups milk
1 bunch chives, minced
Pepper and paprika

Kcal 1153   P 52   G 76 ⚖

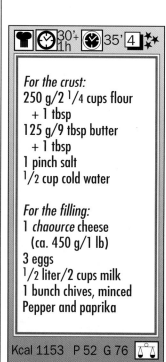

Cheese Choux Puffs

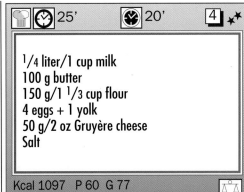

🍳 ⏱ 25'	⏰ 20'	4	✶✶

¹/₄ liter/1 cup milk
100 g butter
150 g/1 ¹/₃ cup flour
4 eggs + 1 yolk
50 g/2 oz Gruyère cheese
Salt

Kcal 1097   P 60 G 77

1 In a saucepan, heat the milk to boiling with a pinch of salt and the butter. Mix in the flour, lower the heat, and cook for 5 minutes, stirring constantly, until the paste comes away from the sides of the pan.

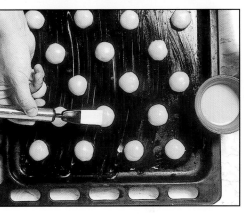

3 Form into small balls, brush with the beaten egg yolk, and arrange on a greased baking sheet. Bake at 170°C/325°F for 20 minutes.

2 Cool. Add the eggs one by one and the diced cheese, mixing well after each addition to obtain a smooth paste.

Vegetables au Gratin ▸

Cover the bottom of an oiled ovenproof dish with alternating, slightly overlapping tomato and zucchini slices. Sprinkle with salt and pepper, the parsley, the shallot, and the herbs. Drizzle with olive oil and bake at 200°C/375°F for 20-30 minutes. Do not allow to brown; if necessary, cover with aluminum foil.

🍳 ⏰ 15' ⏱ 30' 4 ★✦

4 firm, ripe tomatoes
4 zucchini
1 finely minced shallot
1 tsp minced parsley
1 tbsp minced herbs
   (basil, thyme, mint)
2 tbsp olive oil
Salt and pepper

Kcal 63 P 4 G 1 ⚖

Toasted Cheese with Salad

🍳 ⏰ 15' ⏱ 5' 4 ★✦

200 g / ½ lb curly
   endive or oakleaf
   lettuce
4 slices whole wheat
   bread, 1 cm / ½ in
   thick
50 g / 3 ½ tbsp butter
1 *chaource* cheese,
   ca. 400 g
Salt and pepper

For the vinaigrette:
3 tbsp balsamic vinegar
10 tbsp grape seed
   or olive oil
Salt and pepper

Kcal 1079 P 50 G 78 ⚖

Toast the bread to just golden; allow to cool slightly and butter. Cut the cheese into 4 slices.
Place one slice of cheese on each slice of toast and broil in the oven until lightly browned.
Serve on individual plates with a green salad dressed with the balsamic vinaigrette.

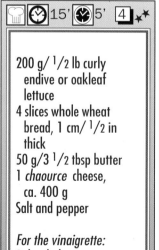

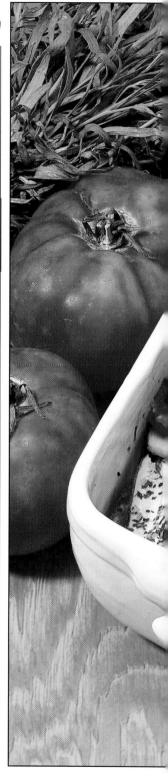

Sautéed Crayfish

B oil the court-bouillon for 3 minutes, then add the crayfish, simmer for 3 minutes, and drain. Clean all the vegetables; slice or dice. Peel the tomato and cut into pieces. Peel the crayfish and reserve the shells.

Sauté the vegetables in 10 g/2 tsp of the butter, add the crayfish, the bouquet garni, half of the wine and $^1/4$ liter/1 cup water, and salt and pepper to taste. Boil the liquid until reduced to $^1/4$ liter/1 cup in all.

Remove the crustaceans from the pan, reserve the vegetables, and strain the fumet. Sauté the reserved vegetables in 10 g/2 tsp butter, pour in the rest of the wine, and cook until reduced by three-quarters.

Add to the fumet and reduce again to half. Strain through a sieve without pressing the vegetables. Beat in the remaining butter with a whisk until light and frothy.

Add the crayfish and the vegetables from the strainer and heat for a few minutes.

Serve sprinkled with fresh tarragon.

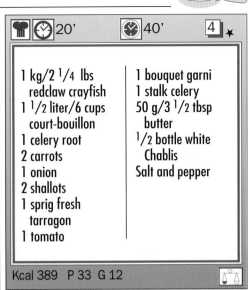

🍳🕐20'   🕑40'   4 ★

1 kg/2 $^1/4$ lbs redclaw crayfish	1 bouquet garni
1 $^1/2$ liter/6 cups court-bouillon	1 stalk celery
1 celery root	50 g/3 $^1/2$ tbsp butter
2 carrots	$^1/2$ bottle white Chablis
1 onion	Salt and pepper
2 shallots	
1 sprig fresh tarragon	
1 tomato	

Kcal 389   P 33   G 12

Crayfish in Wine

P our the wine and the same amount or water into a large pan. Add the salt, the peeled and sliced carrots, the thinly-sliced onion and shallot, the lemon, and the bay leaf, thyme, garlic, parsley, clove, and crushed peppercorns. Bring to a boil; lower the heat and simmer slowly for 30 minutes. Remove from the heat and allow to cool. Replace the pan on high heat. When it returns to boiling, lower the heat and drop in the crayfish. Three minutes after the liquid has returned to boiling, remove the pan from the heat and allow the crayfish to cool in the liquid. With a slotted spoon, transfer the crayfish to a deep serving platter. Remove seasonings from the court-bouillon, leaving only the carrots, onions, and shallots. Pour the liquid and vegetables over the crayfish and serve.

🍶🕐20'   🕑35'   4 ★★

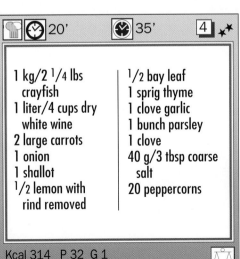

1 kg/2 $^1/4$ lbs crayfish	$^1/2$ bay leaf
1 liter/4 cups dry white wine	1 sprig thyme
2 large carrots	1 clove garlic
1 onion	1 bunch parsley
1 shallot	1 clove
$^1/2$ lemon with rind removed	40 g/3 tbsp coarse salt
	20 peppercorns

Kcal 314   P 32   G 1

◄Crayfish au Gratin

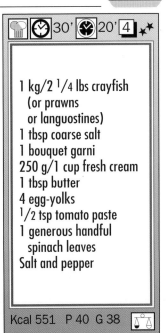

B ring to a boil 3 liters/3 quarts salted water with the bouquet garni. Drop in the crustaceans and cook for 3 minutes; drain, rinse under cold running water, and shell. Sauté the spinach in the butter and reserve.

Beat the egg-yolks with the cream, add the tomato paste, and season to taste with salt and pepper. Cook over low heat, stirring constantly, until the mixture thickens.

Spoon the sauce into individual ovenproof serving dishes, add the crustaceans and spinach, and brown lightly under the oven broiler.

30' 20' 4 ★★

1 kg/2 1/4 lbs crayfish
  (or prawns
  or languostines)
1 tbsp coarse salt
1 bouquet garni
250 g/1 cup fresh cream
1 tbsp butter
4 egg-yolks
1/2 tsp tomato paste
1 generous handful
  spinach leaves
Salt and pepper

Kcal 551   P 40   G 38

Pike with Capers

C lean the mushrooms and skin the shallots; cut both into pieces. Rinse the capers well.

In an oval pan with cover, large enough to hold the fish, melt the butter, add the shallots, and cook until transparent. Add the mushrooms and the capers, mix well, and add salt and pepper to taste.

Gut and scale the fish, season with salt and pepper and lemon juice inside and out, and lay on top of the mixture in the pan.

Cover, and cook over very low heat for 45 minutes.

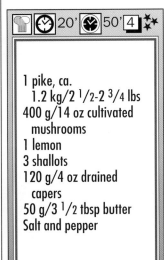

20' 50' 4 ★★

1 pike, ca.
  1.2 kg/2 1/2-2 3/4 lbs
400 g/14 oz cultivated
  mushrooms
1 lemon
3 shallots
120 g/4 oz drained
  capers
50 g/3 1/2 tbsp butter
Salt and pepper

Kcal 332   P 48   G 12

— 23 —

Perch with Walnuts

| 🍳🕐 15' | ❄ 30' | 4 ✦✦ | Kcal 1001 P 36 G 87 | ⚖ |

---

4 perch, ca. 200 g/7 oz each, filleted
200 g/7 oz fresh, salted bacon
50 g/2 oz half walnut meats

Juice of 1 lemon
7 tbsp ($^1/_2$ cup less 1 tbsp) butter + 1 tbsp
Flour

4 tbsp olive oil
1 tbsp minced parsley
Salt and pepper

---

1 Blanch the diced bacon for 1 minute; cool and dry. Salt and pepper the fish and coat lightly with flour. Melt 1 tablespoon butter in 3 tablespoons olive oil in a large skillet. Add the fish and cook over low heat, turning once and basting with the pan juices. When cooked through, sprinkle with lemon juice and keep warm.

2 Sauté the bacon cubes in 1 tablespoon olive oil. Drain on absorbent paper to eliminate the excess fat, then transfer to a clean skillet with 7 tablespoons butter; when the butter begins to foam, add the walnuts and a few drops lemon juice. Arrange the fish on a warmed platter and cover with the hot bacon-and-walnut sauce. Sprinkle with minced parsley and serve with boiled potatoes.

Perch with Champagne Sauce

P lace the cleaned fish in a cast-iron pan together with the garlic, the clove-studded onion, the basil, the bouquet garni, and the champagne. Season with salt and pepper and cook covered over low heat for 30 minutes. Remove the fish from the pan, skin and bone, and set aside on a warmed platter.

Remove the bouquet garni, the basil, the garlic, and the onion and reduce the pan juices. While beating with a whisk, add the butter in small pieces and the lemon juice. Adjust the seasoning. Pour over the fish, sprinkle with the minced parsley, and serve.

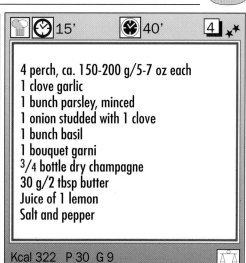

🕐 15'   ⊗ 40'   4 ✦

4 perch, ca. 150-200 g/5-7 oz each
1 clove garlic
1 bunch parsley, minced
1 onion studded with 1 clove
1 bunch basil
1 bouquet garni
3/4 bottle dry champagne
30 g/2 tbsp butter
Juice of 1 lemon
Salt and pepper

Kcal 322 P 30 G 9

Burgundy Fish Stew

🍳⏱ 30'　　🕐 1h　　4 ✸✸　　　　Kcal 1080　P 54　G 37　⚖

1 fillet of pike, 200 g/7 oz	40 g/ $^2/_3$ cup fresh cream	10 potatoes
1 filleted perch, 200 g/7 oz	50 g/3 $^1/_2$ tbsp butter	10 toasted bread rounds rubbed
1 fillet of carp, 200 g/7 oz	50 g/5 $^1/_2$ tbsp flour	with garlic
1 small eel	40 g/1 small onion	1 tbsp minced parsley
12 écrevisses (crayfish)	40 g//1 small carrot	Salt and pepper
6 cloves garlic	40 g/1 $^1/_2$ oz bacon	
1 bottle white Aligoté burgundy	1 bouquet garni	

1 Sauté the diced bacon until golden in a large ungreased stew pot. Add the chopped onion, the sliced carrot, and the crushed garlic and sauté for a minute more. Pour in the white wine and 1 cup water, add salt and pepper and the bouquet garni, and cook this court-bouillon slowly for 30 minutes.

3 Drop all the fish into the pot of simmering court-bouillon and cook for 7-8 minutes. Remove the fish with a skimmer or slotted spoon and set aside on a warmed platter.

2 In another pan, melt the butter and blend in the flour. Pour in $^1/_2$ cup of the court-bouillon and mix until smooth. Set aside. Cut the fish fillets into 4 parts each, shell the écrevisses, and cut the eel into 4 pieces. Steam the potatoes.

4 Strain the court-bouillon into the white sauce pan. Add the cream and simmer until thickened; correct the seasoning. Serve the fish in individual plates, smothered in the sauce and sprinkled with parsley, with the steamed potatoes and the garlic bread rounds.

Salmon in Red Wine Sauce

M elt 70 g/4 1/2 tbsp of the butter, add the finely chopped onions, and cook until golden. Salt and pepper the salmon steaks and place them on top of the onions.
Cover with the red wine and add the bouquet garni. Cook over low heat for about 20 minutes.
Blend the flour into the remaining butter and incorporate, a little at a time, into the salmon pan juices. Remove the bouquet garni, correct the seasoning, and serve.

🍳⏱ 20'   ✷ 30'   4 ★★

4 salmon steaks, 1.5 cm/ 1/4 in thick
2 onions
100 g/7 tbsp butter
1 bottle red wine
1 bouquet garni
1 tbsp flour
Salt and pepper

Kcal 587 P 45 G 31

Trout in Almond-Leek Cream

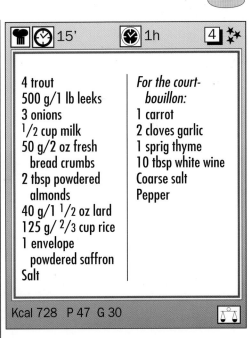

Prepare a court-bouillon con 1 liter/4 cups water and the ingredients listed; remember to wait until the water boils before adding the wine.

Clean, trim, and slice the onions and leeks. Place the trout in a fish braising pan, cover with the boiling court-bouillon, and allow to just simmer for 15-20 minutes according to the size of the fish. Remove the fish from the pan with a slotted spoon and keep warm.

In the meantime, cook the leeks and onions in the melted lard. In a saucepan, dissolve the almond powder in the milk and cook until somewhat thickened. Add the leeks and onions and the crumbled bread. Continue cooking over low heat for 10 minutes, while boiling the rice in salted water.

Drain the rice and place in a saucepan over very low heat. When all the excess moisture has evaporated, pour in a ladleful of court-bouillon in which the saffron has been dissolved. Cover and cook over very low heat for 10 minutes more. Arrange the trout on a heated platter, cover with the leek-and-almond sauce, and serve with the saffron rice on the side.

15'	1h 4

4 trout	*For the court-bouillon:*
500 g/1 lb leeks	
3 onions	1 carrot
$1/2$ cup milk	2 cloves garlic
50 g/2 oz fresh bread crumbs	1 sprig thyme
2 tbsp powdered almonds	10 tbsp white wine
40 g/1 $1/2$ oz lard	Coarse salt
125 g/ $2/3$ cup rice	Pepper
1 envelope powdered saffron	
Salt	

Kcal 728   P 47   G 30

Trout with Mustard Cream

30' 30' 4 Kcal 618 P 40 G 38

1 trout, ca. 1.2 kg/2 1/2 lbs
1/2 bottle white Aligoté burgundy
50 g/3 1/2 tbsp butter
1/5 liter/ 3/4 cup fresh cream
2 tsp smooth prepared mustard
1 carrot
3 shallots
1 sprig tarragon
1 bunch parsley
Salt and pepper

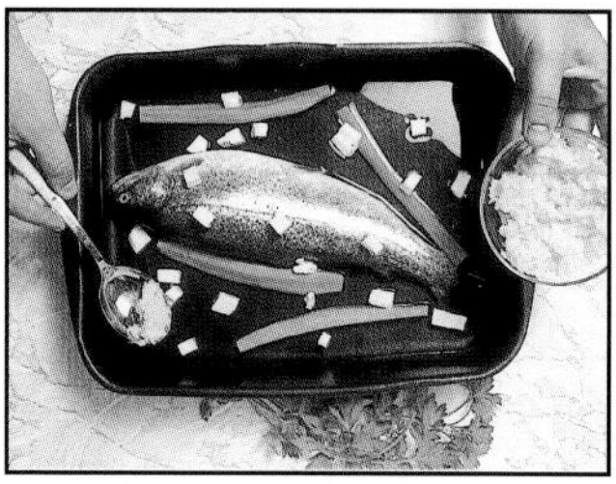

1 Peel the carrot and cut lengthwise into 4 strips. Skin the shallots and chop finely. Season the inside of the trout with salt, pepper, and tarragon. Lay the fish in a baking dish and pour in the wine. Add the butter cut into small pieces, the carrot strips, the shallots, and the parsley. Bake in a preheated 200°C/375°F oven for 15 minutes, basting often with the pan juices. Lower the oven temperature to 160°C/300-325°F and continue baking for 15 minutes longer.

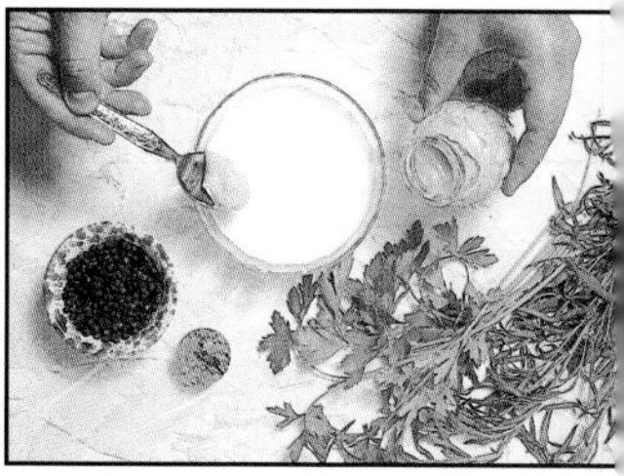

2 Mix the mustard into the cream. Place the cooked trout on a serving platter and drizzle with the mustard cream, sprinkle with salt and pepper, and serve.

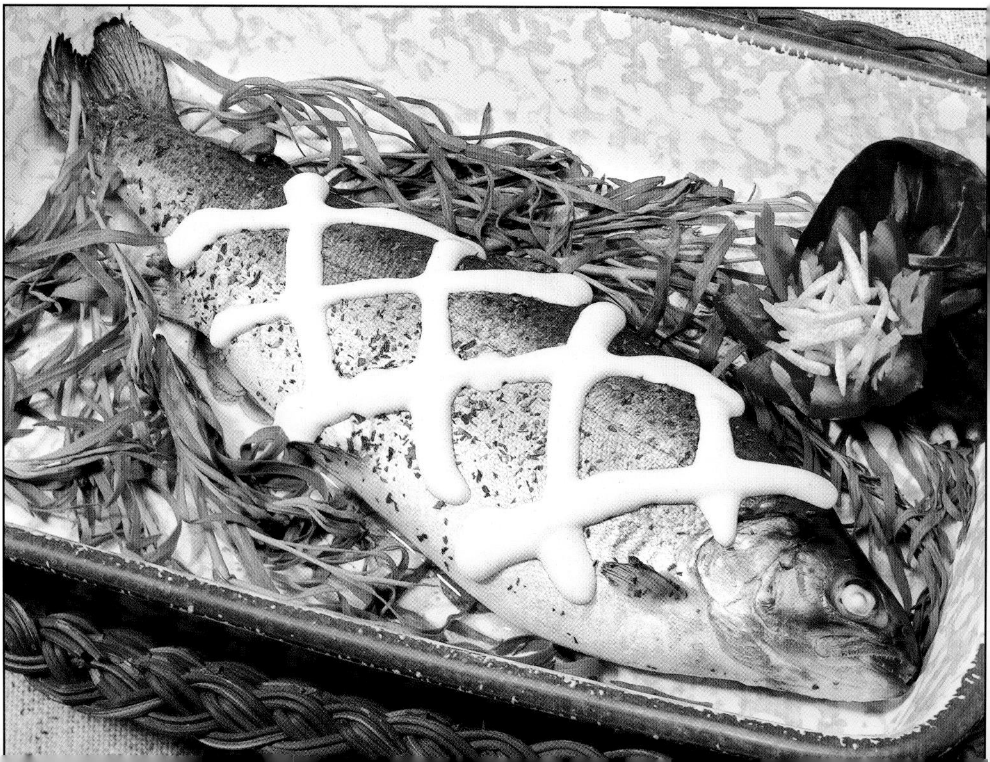

Coq au Vin

Disjoint the chicken; salt and pepper the pieces. Blanch the diced bacon for 2 minutes. Skin the onions. In a large, heavy skillet, melt 2 tablespoons of the butter and sauté the bacon and the onions. Remove from the pan and reserve.

Brown the chicken pieces in the same pan. Heat the *marc*, pour it over the meat, and light.

When the flame has died out, add the bacon and onions, the wine, the bouquet garni, the crushed garlic cloves, and salt and pepper to taste. Cover and cook over low heat for 1 hour.

In the meantime, sauté the mushrooms for 5 minutes in 30 g/2 tbsp of the butter, with a bare sprinkling of salt and pepper, then add the contents of the pan to the chicken. Cook for 1/2 hour longer.

Arrange the chicken pieces, the bacon, the mushrooms, and the onions on a heated platter.

Remove the garlic and the bouquet garni from the cooking pot.

Blend the flour into the remaining butter and add this mixture a little at a time to the pan juices, beating with a whisk until the sauce is velvety. Adjust the salt, pour over the chicken pieces, and serve.

 20'   30'   4 ✲✲   Kcal 1489 P 51 G 113

1 broiler or roasting chicken, 2.5 kg/5 1/2 lbs	20 small white onions	50 g/5 1/2 tbsp flour
200 g/ 1/2 lb lean bacon	250 g/ 1/2 lb small cultivated mushrooms	1/2 shot glass *marc de Bourgogne* (brandy)
1 bottle red wine	1 bouquet garni	Salt and pepper
2 cloves garlic	130 g/9 tbsp butter	

Breast of Duck in Honey Sauce

| 🍳⏱ 20' | ✦ 30' | 4 ★ | Kcal 302   P 28   G 15 | ⚖ |

2 duck breasts, 350 g/12 oz each 2 cooking apples	4 dl/1 ¹/₂ cups cider 2 dl/ ³/₄ cup chicken stock 50 g/3 ¹/₂ tbsp butter	2 tbsp honey Salt and pepper

1 Heat a skillet and cook salted and peppered the duck breasts, without adding any extra fat, for 10 minutes on the skin side and 5 on the other. Transfer from the pan to a cutting board and cover to keep warm.

3 Pour all the fat out of the pan; add the cider, the chicken stock, and salt and pepper. Reduce by half. Add the honey and the butter piece by piece while beating with a whisk. Cut the duck into thickish slices, arrange with the apple slices on heated individual plates, and cover with the hot sauce. Serve immediately.

2 Slice the unpeeled apples and sauté until golden in the duck drippings (10 minutes will suffice). Remove from the pan and reserve.

Rabbit with Mustard

Melt the butter and brown the rabbit, cut into pieces. Season with salt and pepper and add the finely chopped shallots.
Mix the two types of mustard with the white wine and pour over the rabbit. Mix well, lower the heat, cover and cook for 40 minutes, scraping the pan and basting occasionally.
Remove the rabbit pieces and arrange on a warmed platter. Stir the cream into the cooking liquor and pour over the rabbit. Serve immediately.

🍴 🕐 10'   ✹ 45'   4 ✸✸   Kcal 412 P 40 G 19   ⚖

1 rabbit, 1.5 kg/3 1/4 to 3 1/2 lbs	40 g/3 tbsp butter	1 tbsp grainy mustard
2 shallots	4 tbsp dry white wine	3 tbsp fresh cream
	3 tbsp smooth Dijon mustard	Salt and pepper

Rabbit Bourbonnaise

| 🍴⏱ 15' | ⏱ 1h10' | 4 ✦✦ | Kcal 642   P 51   G 37 | ⚖ |

1 rabbit, ca.1.2 kg/2 ¹/₂ lbs	2 cups dry white wine	Salt and pepper
30 g/2 tbsp butter	1 bouquet garni	
¹/₅ liter/ ³/₄ cup heavy cream	12 small round	
2 egg yolks	white onions	
1 tbsp flour	1 tbsp white wine vinegar	

1 Melt the butter in a skillet; add the rabbit (cut into pieces and seasoned with salt and pepper) and the skinned onions and cook over low heat until the meat begins to brown.

2 Dust with the flour, stir well and cook for a few minutes longer. Add the wine, 1 cup water, and the bouquet garni and cook, covered, over low heat for 1 hour. When tender, transfer the rabbit pieces to a heated serving platter.

3 Beat the cream with the egg-yolks and the vinegar, and add to the pan juices while beating vigorously. Pour the sauce over the rabbit pieces and serve.

Marinated Pigeon

🍳⏱ 30' ⏰ 30' 4 ✦✦ Kcal 672 P 42 G 26 ⚖

4 pigeons, 400 g/ca. 1 lb each	1/2 liter/2 cups red wine	1 bouquet garni
50 g/1 medium onion	5 tbsp vinegar	Salt and pepper
50 g/1 medium carrot	5 tbsp *marc de Bourgogne*	
20 g/1 1/2 2 tbsp butter	(brandy)	
40 cl/1 3/4 cups fresh cream	1 clove garlic	

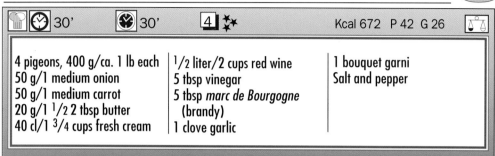

1 Skin and chop the onions; peel and slice the carrots. Place the 4 pigeons in a large bowl with the onions, the carrots, the crushed garlic, the wine, the vinegar, and the bouquet garni. Cover and refrigerate for 5-6 hours.

3 Remove the pigeons and keep warm. Deglaze the pan with the *marc* over low heat. Pour in the strained marinade and reduce by half over high heat.

2 Remove the pigeons from the marinade, dry, and rub with salt and pepper inside and out. Brown in 20 g/1 1/2 tbsp of the butter in an ovenproof pan. Bake at 200°C/375°F for 20-25 minutes.

4 Lower the heat, add the cream and cook until the sauce reaches a smooth, creamy consistency. Adjust the seasoning. Serve the pigeons cut into quarters and smothered in the sauce.

Hen in Cream

🍳⏱ 15' ⏲ 45' [4] ✦✦ Kcal 1687 P 47 G 147 ⚖

1 hen, 1.5-2 kg/3 1/2 to 4 1/2 lbs	1 onion	1/5 liter/ 3/4 cup dry white wine
1 liter/4 cups fresh cream	10 medium cultivated mushrooms	1 bouquet garni
100 g/6 tbsp butter	2 cloves garlic	Salt and pepper

1 Disjoint the hen; use only the two single breasts, the legs, the thighs, and the wings. Melt the butter in a capacious skillet, and add the pieces of hen. Season with salt and pepper.

3 Cook the hen pieces for 6-7 minutes per side. Deglaze the pan with the wine and reduce the cooking liquid.

2 Add the quartered onion, the sliced mushrooms, the unpeeled garlic cloves, and the bouquet garni.

4 Pour in the cream. Simmer for 30 minutes longer, then remove the pan from the heat. Transfer the meat to a deep serving dish. Strain the pan juices and whip in the blender. Correct the seasoning and pour over the hen pieces. Serve hot.

Poularde in Terracotta

1 young hen,1.5-1.8 kg/3 1/4 to 4 lbs	6 tbsp flour	*For the marinade:*
60 g/4 tbsp butter	1 bouquet garni	1 bottle sparkling white wine (Crémant)
500 g/1 lb cultivated mushrooms, sliced	Salt and pepper	1 large carrot, sliced
		1 large onion, sliced

Remove the giblets from the hen and reserve. Salt and pepper the inside of the bird and marinate, refrigerated, for 4 hours with the carrot, onion, and wine, stirring often.

Place an ovenproof dish upside down on the bottom of a deep, round ovenproof terracotta pot large enough to hold the hen.

Pour 40 cl/1 3/4 cup of the marinade into the pot and set the hen on the dish, above the level of the liquid. Knead the flour with a little water; roll the paste into a rope long enough to seal the cover of the pot. Bake at 190°C/375°F for 1 1/2 hours.

Sauté the giblets in 15 g/1 tbsp of the butter, then add the bouquet garni and the marinade. Boil until the liquid has evaporated, then add 1/3 liter/1 1/3 cups water and reduce by half over low heat. Remove the bouquet garni. Put the solid ingredients through a food mixer; reserve with the pan juices.

Sauté the mushrooms in 45 g/3 tbsp butter; when they have expelled all their liquid, add the reserved ingredients and cook slowly for 3-4 minutes longer. At the end of the baking time, break the seal on the pot and extract the hen.

Serve on a platter with the mushrooms; serve the pot drippings separately.

Chicken with Mustard

Cut the chicken into 8 pieces; rub with salt, pepper, and the paprika.

Sauté the chicken pieces until golden in the melted butter, then cover the skillet and cook over low heat for $1/2$ hour. Transfer the chicken to an ovenproof serving dish.

Skim off the excess grease from the cooking pan, return to the heat, and deglaze with the wine. Add the grated cheese and stir until melted. Pour in the cream, heat to just boiling, and stir in the mustard.

Pour the sauce over the chicken pieces, sprinkle with the breadcrumbs, and brown under the broiler in a hot oven for about 15 minutes.

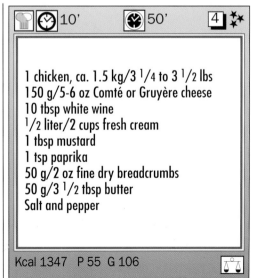

🍳⏱ 10'   ❄ 50'   4 ✵✵

1 chicken, ca. 1.5 kg/3 $1/4$ to 3 $1/2$ lbs
150 g/5-6 oz Comté or Gruyère cheese
10 tbsp white wine
$1/2$ liter/2 cups fresh cream
1 tbsp mustard
1 tsp paprika
50 g/2 oz fine dry breadcrumbs
50 g/3 $1/2$ tbsp butter
Salt and pepper

Kcal 1347 P 55 G 106

Lamb Parmentier

🍴⏱ 1h	⏰ 35'	4 ⭐⭐	Kcal 582 P 62 G 25	⚖

1 kg/2 1/4 lbs boned saddle of lamb 500 g/1 lb potatoes	125 g/ 1/4 lb *époisses* cheese 2 tbsp olive oil 15 tbsp milk	20 g/1 1/2 tbsp butter 2 cloves garlic Salt and pepper

1 Cut 4 filets in the saddle of lamb and reserve. Cut the remaining meat into chunks, season with salt and pepper, and sauté in 1 tablespoon olive oil. Allow to cool, then chop finely.

2 Peel and boil the potatoes and put them through a fine vegetable mill. Whip in the milk and the butter. Add the chopped cheese, whipping until completely melted. Season with salt and pepper.

3 Spread half the potatoes in a buttered ovenproof serving dish, cover with the chopped meat, and top with the remaining potatoes. Season the lamb filets with salt and pepper and sauté for 7-8 minutes in 1 tablespoon olive oil. Remove the pan from the heat. Transfer the meat to a heated dish and cover with aluminum foil. Pour off the fat from the pan, pour in 1/4 liter/1 cup water, add the peeled and crushed garlic cloves, and bring to a boil. Cook, scraping the bottom of the pan, until only a few spoonfuls of liquid remain. Brown the Parmentier under the oven broiler for 4-5 minutes and serve together with the thinly-sliced lamb filets topped with the strained garlic sauce.

Marinated Lamb Noisettes

Prepare the marinade. Cut the two lamb loins (*noisettes*) into 8 pieces (2 per serving) and leave to marinate in a cool place for 24 hours.

🍴⏱ 15'+24h	⏰ 1h	4 ★★

2 lamb *noisettes*
(the meaty part of the loin of lamb)
1 beef or lamb bone
5 tbsp olive oil

For the marinade:
3 carrots, sliced
2 onions, quartered
1 clove garlic, crushed
1/2 liter/2 cups white wine
1 sprig thyme
1 bay leaf
1 bunch parsley

For the sauce:
10 tbsp beef stock
5 tbsp vinegar
1/4 liter/1 cup fresh cream
2 tbsp port wine
1 tsp flour
1 tbsp light mustard
70 g/2-3 oz veal liver, in one slice
2 tsp butter

Kcal 618 P 42 G 36

The next day, remove the carrots, the onions and the garlic from the marinade; drain and dry the meat thoroughly. Reserve the liquid. Saute the meat with the bone in 2 tablespoons olive oil until they begin to color; dust with the flour, stir well, and continue cooking until golden. Pour in the vinegar and continue to cook, stirring, for a few minutes. Add the marinade and the beef stock slowly, lower the heat, and continue cooking for 45 minutes. Put the sauce through a vegetable mill into another pan. Add the cream and bring to a boil.

Add the port wine and remove the pan from the heat and let stand. Sauté the slice of liver for a minute or two in the melted butter (it should remain pink), then chop in a food mixer with the mustard. Add the reserved sauce, stir briefly, and then heat for a minute or two over low heat. Strain through the vegetable mill and keep warm.

Sauté the *noisettes* until golden in the remaining oil. Serve on a heated platter smothered in the sauce.

Pheasant with Grapes

🍳⏱ 20'	⏲ 1h	4 ⁜		Kcal 539 P 51 G 18	⚖

1 young hen pheasant, ca.1.2 kg/2 ¹/₂ lbs 250 g/ ¹/₂ lb shallots 500 g/1 lb white and purple	grapes ¹/₂ liter/2 cups red wine 3 juniper berries 3 tbsp olive oil	1 tbsp butter 1 bouquet garni Salt and pepper

Melt the butter with the olive oil in a cast iron skillet. Sauté the sliced shallots with the disjointed pheasant until the meat is golden brown all over. Pour off the fat from the pan; add the wine, the juniper berries, and the bouquet garni, and season with salt and pepper. Cover and cook over low heat for 1 hour. Five minutes before the end of the cooking time, add the grapes and adjust the seasoning. Remove the bouquet garni. Serve the meat and grapes in the pan juices.

Veal Kidneys in Wine

2 veal kidneys with the fat and membrane removed
100 g/ $^1/_4$ lb smoked bacon
12 cultivated mushrooms
110 g/7 tbsp butter
2 shallots
10 tbsp white Aligoté burgundy
20 tbsp chicken stock
1 tbsp cooking cream
1 tbsp minced parsley
Salt and pepper

Kcal 720   P 38   G 50

2 Cut the kidneys into 1.5 cm/$^3/_4$ in slices; season with salt and pepper. Melt 50 g/3 $^1/_2$ tbsp of the butter and cook the kidney slices for 4 minutes per side over high heat. Drain over a strainer. Pour off the cooking fat.

1 Dice the bacon and place in a saucepan covered with cold water. Bring to a boil and cook for 5 minutes. Drain the bacon and rinse under cold running water; drain again and dry. Melt 1 $^1/_2$ tablespoons of the butter in a frying pan and sauté the bacon cubes until golden; remove from the heat and keep warm. Preheat the oven to 150°C/300°F. Clean the mushrooms, cut into quarters, and cook for about 10 minutes in 20 g/1 $^1/_2$ tablespoons of the butter. Reserve and keep warm.

3 In the same pan, cook the shallots with the wine until the liquid has completely evaporated. Pour in the chicken stock and reduce by half; finally, blend in the cooking cream and the butter, a piece at a time, while beating with a whisk. Strain the sauce, add salt if needed, and keep warm over hot water. Heat the kidney slices for 3 minutes in a hot oven. Arrange in 4 individual plates, top with the sauce, and surround with the mushrooms and bacon. Sprinkle with the minced parsley and serve.

Chablis Ham

Melt 1 tablespoon butter and sauté the minced shallots until transparent. Pour in the wine and the vinegar; raise the heat and boil uncovered until reduced by half. Add the crushed tomatoes and season with salt and pepper; simmer for 15 minutes.

Melt the rest of the butter in a large skillet and heat the ham slices, turning once.

When the sauce has cooked for 15 minutes, add the cream and adjust the seasoning. Heat for 2-3 minutes without boiling; remove from the heat.

Arrange the ham slices in a baking pan, cover with the sauce, and bake in a preheated 250°C/475°F oven for 15 minutes. Serve piping hot.

15' 45' 4 ★★

4 slices cooked ham, 1/2 cm/ 1/4 in thick
60 g/2-3 oz shallots
150 g/ 3/4 cup crushed tomatoes
15 tbsp fresh cream
2 tbsp butter
1/3 bottle white Chablis
15 tbsp white wine vinegar
Salt and pepper

Kcal 694   P 19   G 48

Pork Casserole

🧑‍🍳 ⏰ 20 ⏲ 1h 40 | 68 ✦✦

800 g/1 ³/₄ lbs pork
  breast, diced
800 g/1 ³/₄ lbs potatoes
4 onions
30 g/2 tbsp butter
1 tbsp olive oil
15 juniper berries
¹/₂ cup white wine
Salt and pepper

Kcal 635 P 43 G 23 ⚖

Melt the butter with the olive oil over low heat in a cast-iron or copper casserole with cover. Taking care that the butter does not darken, make a layer of thinly-sliced potatoes, one of pork, and one of thinly-sliced onions. Season each layer with salt and pepper and a few juniper berries. Continue in this manner until all the ingredients are used up. Pour in the wine and ¹/₂ cup hot water. Cover and cook over low heat for ¹/₂ hour.

Transfer the casserole to a preheated 180°C/350°F oven and continue cooking for 1 ¹/₄ hours.

Boeuf Bourguignonne

1.5 kg/3 ¹/₂ lbs stew beef, cubed	2 onions	thyme, bay leaf)
50 g/3 ¹/₂ tbsp butter	30 g/ ¹/₄ cup flour	Salt and pepper
5 tbsp olive oil	2 cloves garlic	
100 g/ ¹/₄ lb fresh bacon	1 ¹/₂ bottles red burgundy wine	
2 carrots	1 bouquet garni (parsley, leek,	

1. In stew pot (preferably earthenware), brown the diced bacon and the beef in the butter and olive oil with the sliced onions and carrots.

3. Remove the meat, the garlic, and the bouquet garni, and if necessary reduce the cooking liquid to a good consistency. Replace the meat in the sauce, adjust the salt to taste, and serve.

2. Dust with the flour, stir, and cover with the wine. Add the crushed garlic, the bouquet garni, and salt and pepper. Cover and cook over very low heat for 2 ¹/₂ hours.

Pear and Blueberry "Clafoutis"

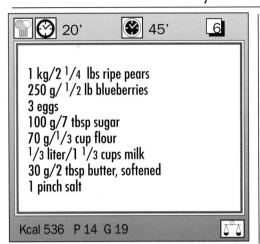

🍳⏱ 20' ✹ 45' 6

1 kg/2 ¹/₄ lbs ripe pears
250 g/ ¹/₂ lb blueberries
3 eggs
100 g/7 tbsp sugar
70 g/¹/₃ cup flour
¹/₃ liter/1 ¹/₃ cups milk
30 g/2 tbsp butter, softened
1 pinch salt

Kcal 536   P 14   G 19

Place the flour, sugar, and salt in a bowl stir in the beaten eggs. Beat until light then add the milk and the softened butter and continue beating until well-blended.

Peel the pears and cut in half lengthwise rinse the blueberries.

Arrange the fruit in the bottom of a buttered baking dish, cover with the batter, and bake in a preheated 180°C/350°F oven for 45 minutes.

Pear "Corniottes"

Cut a thin slice off the bottom of each pear; do not remove the stems. Simmer the pears for 30 minutes with the wine, sugar, and cinnamon. Cool the fruit in the syrup. Roll out the puff paste and divide into 8 parts. Spread each pear with 1/2 teaspoon honey and wrap in a square of puff paste. Brush with the beaten egg, stand in a buttered baking dish, and bake at 200°C/375°F for 15-20 minutes until golden brown. Turn off the oven and allow the pears to cool slowly near the open oven door.

30' 50' 4

8 small pears
1 liter/4 cups red Mâcon wine
400 g/2 cups sugar
1 tbsp ground cinnamon
1 kg/2 1/4 lbs prepared puff paste
4 tsp creamy honey
1 egg for glazing

Kcal 2014 P 17 G 109

Spice Bread Cream Loaf

🍳🕐 30'	⏱ 15'	4		Kcal 1380 P 33 G 47	⚖

1 spice bread (*pain d'épices*)	*For the walnut cream:*	25 g/1 oz walnut meats
200 g/7 oz pitted dried prunes	4 egg-yolks	*For the syrup:*
50 g/3 1/2 tbsp sugar	100 g/7 tbsp sugar	1/2 cup rum
50 g/2 oz honey	125 g/9 tbsp butter	50 g/3 1/2 tbsp sugar

1 Cook the prunes with the sugar, the honey, and 10 tablespoons water for 15 minutes over low heat, then purée in a food blender. Reserve.

3 Dissolve the 50 g/3 1/2 tbsp sugar in the rum and a few teaspoons water, without heating. Cut the *pain d'épices* into 1/2 cm/1/4 in slices.

2 Dissolve the 100 g/7 tbsp sugar in a little water; heat to boiling. Beat the egg-yolks with an electric mixer and then beat in the sugar syrup. When cool, blend in the softened butter and the walnuts.

4 Line a loaf pan with waxed paper or baking paper. Cover the bottom with a layer of *pain d'épices*, drizzle with the rum syrup, and cover with the puréed prunes. Make another layer of *pain d'épices*, rum syrup, and walnut cream. Continue until the ingredients are used up. Unmold and serve as is or with a chocolate glaze: melt a few squares of semisweet chocolate over hot water and stir in one tablespoon oil. Mix until smooth, allow to cool somewhat, and spread over the cake.

White Peaches in Ratafia

Peel and remove the stones from the peaches; cut into quarters. Melt the butter in a saucepan, add the peaches, and sprinkle over the sugar. Cook over low heat for 8 minutes, turning the fruit frequently but delicately in order to avoid breaking the pieces. Allow to caramelize lightly.

Pour in the ratafia and continue cooking, again over low heat, for 5 minutes more.

Remove the peaches carefully and arrange on a deep platter. Add the minced tarragon to the cooking juices and reduce by half.

Pour the sauce over the peach quarters and serve warm or cold.

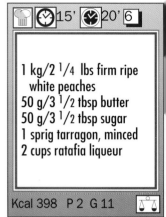

15' 20' 6

1 kg/2 1/4 lbs firm ripe white peaches
50 g/3 1/2 tbsp butter
50 g/3 1/2 tbsp sugar
1 sprig tarragon, minced
2 cups ratafia liqueur

Kcal 398   P 2   G 11

Pears in Cassis

🎩 🕐 20' ⏱ 30' 6️⃣

6 Williams pears
50 g/3 ¹/₂ tbsp sugar
1 liter/4 cups red wine
¹/₂ cup *crème de cassis*
(black currant liqueur)
1 stick cinnamon

Kcal 654 P 1 G 1 ⚖️

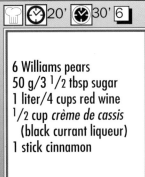

Peel the pears but do not remove the stem. Stand the pears upright in a saucepan, pour in the wine and one-third of the crème de cassis, add the sugar and the cinnamon stick. Bring to a boil, cover, lower the heat, and cook at a bare simmer for 30 minutes.
Remove the pears from the pan and stand in a fairly deep serving dish. Reduce the cooking liquid by half, filter, add the rest of the liqueur, and pour the sauce over the fruit. This dessert is usually served cold.

Baked Candied Apples

1 Rinse and core the apples. Cut off the tops and set aside. Arrange the apples in a non-stick baking pan, sprinkle with the honey, and bake in a slow 80°C/175°F oven for 1 hour to candy them. Allow to cool.

3 Divide the pastry into 8 parts and roll out each to a 3 by 10 cm (1 ¼ by 4 in) rectangle, ½ cm/ ¼ in thick. Allow to stand in a warm place.

2 Dissolve the yeast in the warmed milk. Process with the flour, egg, salt, and the butter cut into small pieces, for 3 minutes in a food mixer.

4 Warm the honey in a saucepan. Grate the rind of the lemon, squeeze the juice, and mix both with the cream and the egg yolks Pour this mixture into the honey in the saucepan, mix well, and cook for a few minutes over low heat, stirring constantly. Spread the pastry with the honey cream; wind one strip around the base of each apple, and brush with the beaten egg. Butter an oven proof dish and stand the wrapped apples in it Place one grape inside each apple; replace the tops. Dust with the confectioners' suga and bake at 150°C/325°F for 1 hour.

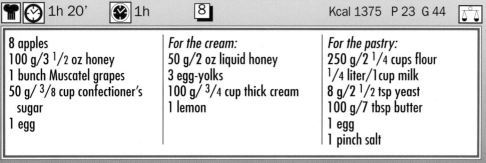

🍳 ⏱ 1h 20'   ⏲ 1h   8   Kcal 1375 P 23 G 44 ⚖

8 apples	*For the cream:*	*For the pastry:*
100 g/3 ^{1}/$_2$ oz honey	50 g/2 oz liquid honey	250 g/2 ^{1}/$_4$ cups flour
1 bunch Muscatel grapes	3 egg-yolks	^{1}/$_4$ liter/1 cup milk
50 g/ ^{3}/$_8$ cup confectioner's	100 g/ ^{3}/$_4$ cup thick cream	8 g/2 ^{1}/$_2$ tsp yeast
sugar	1 lemon	100 g/7 tbsp butter
1 egg		1 egg
		1 pinch salt

Cheese Pie Bresse Style

Use part of the dough to make a disk $^1/_2$ cm/ $^1/_4$ in thick. Place on a buttered baking sheet and allow to rise for about 2 hours at room temperature. With the rest of the dough, braid a rope the length of the circumference of the disk and about 1 cm/ $^1/_2$ in thick; brush with beaten egg and "glue" onto the edge of the disk. Blend the cheese, the sugar, the whole egg plus one yolk, and the sifted flour and beat until smooth. Prick the risen dough all over with a fork; spread with the cheese mixture, making sure it covers the whole surface.
Bake at 190°C/375°F for about 20 minutes, checking that the pie is cooked through and browned before removing from the oven and serving.

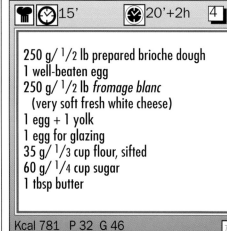

15'   20'+2h   4

250 g/ $^1/_2$ lb prepared brioche dough
1 well-beaten egg
250 g/ $^1/_2$ lb *fromage blanc*
   (very soft fresh white cheese)
1 egg + 1 yolk
1 egg for glazing
35 g/ $^1/_3$ cup flour, sifted
60 g/ $^1/_4$ cup sugar
1 tbsp butter

Kcal 781   P 32   G 46

Cherry Cobbler

Place the flour, sugar, and salt in a bowl. Make a well in the center and incorporate the eggs one by one. Add the rum, the milk, and 100 g/6 1/2tbsp melted butter. Beat the batter until smooth. Butter a deep pie pan. Place the unpitted cherries on the bottom; dot with 20 g/1 1/2 tbsp butter cut into small pieces; cover with the batter. Bake at 210°C/400°F for 25 minutes. Dust with the vanilla sugar and serve.

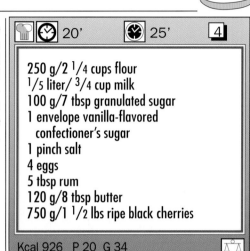

🍴⏱ 20'   ✺ 25'   4

250 g/2 1/4 cups flour
1/5 liter/ 3/4 cup milk
100 g/7 tbsp granulated sugar
1 envelope vanilla-flavored
   confectioner's sugar
1 pinch salt
4 eggs
5 tbsp rum
120 g/8 tbsp butter
750 g/1 1/2 lbs ripe black cherries

Kcal 926 P 20 G 34

Stewed Peaches

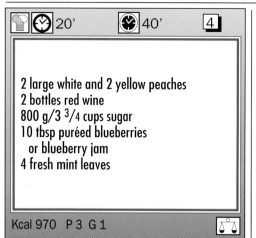

🕐 20'   ⏱ 40'   4

2 large white and 2 yellow peaches
2 bottles red wine
800 g/3 ³/₄ cups sugar
10 tbsp puréed blueberries
 or blueberry jam
4 fresh mint leaves

Kcal 970 P 3 G 1

Prepare this dessert at least 12 hours before serving.

Peel the peaches. Heat the wine and the sugar in a saucepan over low heat; when it just begins to simmer, add the peaches, cover and cook over very low heat for 30 minutes. Allow the peaches to cool in the sauce, then add the blueberry purée or jam and refrigerate. Serve the next day.

Champagne Rose Jam

G ather or purchase 100 g/3 $^1/_2$ to 4 oz rose petals. Place in a colander and immerse very rapidly twice in cold water, in order to rinse the petals without altering their fragrance. Drain and lay out to dry.

Pour the 500 g/2 $^1/_4$ cups sugar and the same amount of water into a large, heavy enamel or stainless steel pan, bring to a boil, and remove from the heat. Drop in the rose petals and allow to cool to room temperature.

Remove the petals with a slotted spoon, heat the syrup to boiling, remove from the heat, add the petals again, and allow to cool. Repeat this operation 5 times.

Prepare another syrup with 400 g/ $^7/_8$ cup sugar and 200 g/ $^3/_4$ cup water and add the first syrup with the petals. Bring to a boil, add the remaining sugar, 100 g/ $^3/_8$ cup water,

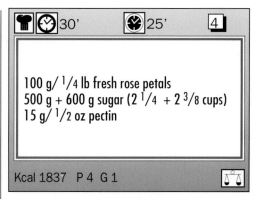

🍴🕐 30' ⚜ 25' 4

100 g/ $^1/_4$ lb fresh rose petals
500 g + 600 g sugar (2 $^1/_4$ + 2 $^3/_8$ cups)
15 g/ $^1/_2$ oz pectin

Kcal 1837   P 4   G 1

and the pectin. Cook over low heat, stirring gently, for a few minutes.

The jam is ready when a drop placed on a cold plate jells immediately.

Index of recipes

COOKING IN BURGUNDY AND CHAMPAGNE

Project and editorial concept: Casa Editrice Bonechi
Series Editor: Alberto Andreini
Editor: Paolo Piazzesi
Graphics and cover: Maria Rosanna Malagrinò
Layout: Marina Miele
Edited by: Patrizia Chirichigno
English translation by: Paula Boomsliter

All the recipes in this book have been tested by our team of chefs.
In the kitchen: Lisa Mugnai
Nutritionist: Dr. John Luke Hili

The photographs of the foods, property of the Bonechi Archives, were taken by Andrea Fantauzzo.

© by CASA EDITRICE BONECHI, Florence – Italy
e-mail: bonechi@bonechi.it
website: www.bonechi.it – www.bonechi.com

* * *